Praise for
Balance of Delicate Things

Balance of Delicate Things by Peg Codding
is a perfect complement to your mood, your
state of mind. Her pieces will resonate with
you, and enlighten, moving you through
nostalgia, heartache, and joy. Care is given
to the little moments we can overlook, and
her ruminations are a breath of fresh air.
Grace is offered to life's challenging moments,
including those that touch your own trauma or
healing. Here, Codding offers you permission
to be gentle with yourself.

> — Marissa Forbes, Author of *Surviving Peter Pan*
> and *Brief and Bleeding Margins*

Balance of Delicate Things is a solemn,
reflective poetry collection that is true to the
human experience. Peg Codding writes on the
realities of personal pain while finding healing
in the beauty of the American Southwest, also
in the loving kindness of others. This book
ultimately demonstrates that it is never too
early to hurt, and never too late to heal.

> — María Toloché, Author of *Sassafras Road*

This collection by Peg Codding strikes that impossibly delicate balance: within violence, Peg reminds us that we can find peace. We can breathe deep and become one with the stillness of the morning. In that stillness, we can finally become. Peg's collection is important for women in the West and for any woman who has known truly seismic pain.

— Cecily Stone, Author of *These Chasms in the Earth*

Balance of Delicate Things is a thoughtful gift to the reader, an offering of memory, gratitude, and beauty that allows one to receive what another gives. Peg Codding's poetry is a gentle journey, a road trip through the self with stops in childhood, loss, love, music, and beautiful Wyoming. This collection waits for you until you need it most, again and again.

— Marie Timbreza, MAT, Author of *Sustenance: 50 Poems + One Love Story*

Balance of Delicate Things

Balance of Delicate Things

Poems by
Peg Codding

Balance of Delicate Things
© 2024 Peg Codding
ISBN: 979-8-9917306-0-0
Library of Congress Control Number: 2024922511

Cover Art © Ronald Reed Sill

First Edition, 2024

Published in Longmont, Colorado
Printed in the United States of America

Edited by Laura Joy Clarke
Cover Design by Kayla Toris
Layout Design by Kimberly James & Emily Anne Evans

Published with the assistance of CLI Books

To Jeffrey, who brings me coffee every morning, and sings to me when he places the warm cup into my hands.

To Sue Ann and John, who brought me to myself, and stayed to witness the person I've become.

To my brother David and my sister Mary, whose paths have brought them to courage.

To Donna Kausek who opened her door to me, the first of many to open.

To Chaco, my African Grey, who sat on my shoulder while I wrote, chirping suggestions.

Contents

Centering: Nature's Promise

Being in the Delicate

Watching the World

Finding Perspective

"And she planted her poetry everywhere,
so it could flower,
in even the most unlikely places."
I met her once, walking in the mountains.
She was planting her poems
alongside the wildflowers.

We stood in silence listening
to the mountain and the trees
whose voices you can hear in the wind.
I still see her now and then,
as she slips a poem
into the slipper of a ballerina
or onto the bow of a violinist.

And at night she whispers in my ear.

— J.S. Woodward

Preface

This collection is for anyone who knows the struggle that comes in falling and in getting up again, along with the joy of living with intention.

Rainer Maria Rilke said of life, "Let everything happen to you, beauty and terror. Just keep going. No feeling is final."[1] Frederick Buechner said of being, "Here in the world, beautiful and terrible things will happen. Don't be afraid."[2] Letting life in is not a choice. Living it mindfully, is.

My life is a balance of delicate things. There is peace, suffering, joy, compassion, sorrow and strength. I live in the delicate, wanting balance, but also surprise in the unexpected. In what comes, I respond, change, succeed, sometimes fail. These poems reflect these moments.

We all know trauma; I am no exception. Selected poems speak to the violence I experienced before recovery brought me to myself. I came from a childhood with violence in it. Removed from it then, I returned to it for a while as an adult. This is not uncommon among survivors. We do what we learn. These times are behind me now.

There are a few poems here about loss by death, about gratitude gained. I lost my sister during the writing of these poems, and a best friend. Finally, this collection includes work about things observed beyond myself. I invite you to read about beauty, spirit, music, history and creativity, all things loved.

I wrote some of these poems while physically separated from the events of domestic violence. These were reflections of my moments of reckoning. I often wrote late at night or in early morning, usually by candlelight. In these hours, words often came when sleep would not. Some poems were written longhand at an old table on a closed-in porch under a New England moon. This beautiful colonial home stands on the edge of conservation land in historic Concord, Massachusetts. Others were written amid boxes in a city apartment in Boston. There I scribbled words on paper when the silence of my solitary life felt deafening.

Some poems were written in difficult moments and reflect it; others while I was at peace with my own heart's beating. I remember everything about the writing, who I was, and what I was feeling. It took time for me to know where I was going. I grew into a sweet life, living and writing among the western mountains of my youth. These mountains feed me, and will forever remain at the center of my soul.

The content in the collection is ordered, at times, across topics. Lighter poems are infused among more challenging ones to allow for a cleansing of the reader's palate. There are a few poems followed by a QR code so that you can listen to the music referenced in the poem. This works when the reader holds the cell phone camera up to the code and clicks on the link that pops up.

I invite you into these pages of my life, into a *Balance of Delicate Things*.

Balance of Delicate Things

Losing and Finding

"You are not a drop in the ocean.
You are the entire ocean in a drop."

Rumi

Drawing of Jeffrey Heartlove by Tatum Jones

Ode to Childhood

Jeffrey Heartlove
(about my cat)
by Tatum Jones, Age 8

lazy
chubby
old

"cudly"
cute

likes to play

name Jeff

black
white
gray

greenish
blue
eyes

very
sleepy.

Haiku #1

Green earth of summer.
Children laughing while swinging.
Hope, the sound they make.

Tears

To Michael

"Why do we have so many tears?"
he said looking up into my eyes.
He was sitting on an ottoman
leaning forward
in a stream of sadness.
Eyes, windows of pain.

Beside him, in his bed, she lay
breathing in the rhythm of the dying —
her eyes toward the heavens,
body yet unwilling to take flight.
Hearing is the last of our senses
to leave us. Her dog knows this
as he pants and barks
his presence in her room.

Candles burning, Rosary spoken.
Psalms read. She hears
her playlist on her phone.
Voices in her room are
those of sons grown,
now home together,
talking with each other
in a way brothers do.

Our motion and emotion
keep her lingering —
but she is between lives.
Eyes, she sees past us,
almost to heaven —
a heaven hoped for, but not yet home.
Does she approach the open door,
then stop? Is she looking back?
Her eyes speak this possibility.
Is she reaching for him one last time,
for us too, to hold us into eternity?

We tell her we will be ok —
(perhaps so we'll believe it).
We talk to her,
arrange her covers on the bed,
touch her skin as if to memorize.
We sit and lie with her
and feel her fading warmth.

But how do we continue holding
her life in ours?
How do we hold her loss
in our hands?
"Why do we have so many tears?"
her husband asks.
Looking into his weeping eyes,
I answer, *"Because we need them."*

Chasing Loss

To Jeffrey

In your pain —

your anticipation of losing her —

> I chase you
> to hold you

as you run away
in search of the safe space
in the deepest corner of your mind.

Haiku #2

You look in my eyes
Sun rises warm on my face.
Soul smiles. Day begins.

Sunflowers

To Jeffrey

Love. You knock over sunflowers in a vase by
the window. Water and circles of yellow fly,
sailing across the floor, destination certain.
In a splash, they land, loud and hard, but the
floor is forgiving. My solitude is disrupted as
you yell briefly at the flowers, the mess, or at a
force unseen, but deeply felt. Like water your
pain flows, splashing wildly, but with gravity.
Pain cries out at the unexpected. The death
vigil ages those who love without reservation.
Your anger races toward heaven. No recourse,
it quietly descends into reality. Looking at the
floor, what flows are the tears of flowers, but
also your own.

Silently, I arrange the golden disks, returning
flowers to vase. I set them by the window,
again in sunlight. The flowers breathe,
recovering from their fall. Your recovery is less
easy. Reaching deep into beauty, each flower
shows its face, reaching out to touch your
silence. Do you notice their efforts? I wish I
could return her to you, but some things broken
shatter under heaven, lost without reconcile.

In their silent sunning, the flowers offer presence and calm. They are whole again. They've learned to smile in adversity and must survive because we need them to. Beauty is hope.

In a moment's passing, I say, "Honey, it's ok," but I know it isn't. Your face unshaven, hair falling in your eyes, this ritual is grief crying. Your expression, open to translation, needs none. Alone, looking down at chaos, you clearly feel it within. You touch it there, while looking past me. Your eyes don't reach for mine. Your language is anger, grief. Silence, your being. How can you accept that your sister, your heart's beating, is beyond your reach, but by memory?

But, sunflowers are wise in their way. They can seek you out, and do. Their golden petals are loving hands reaching from beauty for your soul. They speak silently in their soothing, as if to say. . .

". . .you are not alone.

We. Are Here."

Loss

Too much.
Wake up.
Hits you hard.

Dream.
Finds you there.

Soul.
Smothered in it.

Heart pulses pain.
You are always
a target for it.
No hiding.

Life means death.
Death is all around us.
Can see it —
touch its searching fingers.
Pain is a heavy
silent scream.

Love is dying.
(Love dies.)

Mortality just is.
Acceptance isn't.

DEATH

It looks you in the eye —
cold hard stare, no tears.
Says, "Just try to stop me.
I'm taking what is mine."
Your life is mine. Always has been.

Just a time thing. I'll choose.
The hand I play always wins.
No odds. You bet time.
Foolishly. Your people are mine too.
If you love, you will lose. Choose.

Your hands' releasing is goodbye.
I am not your friend;
I am your reality. Cannot hide.
I am your death.
My time, often untimely.
Look within.
You'll find me always lurking.

I was here before you.
Hereafter too. Death —
your birthright.
My right to exercise.
My eyes are the eyes of fate.

Yours.

Balance of Delicate Things

My walk in the world is a balance
of delicate things —
left and right turns,
mountains, craters —
living on the edge
of beauty and terror.

Once I ran, silent on a bitter night.
Small child, I held the hand of one
parent to escape the other.
My heart beat to the chill
of violence.

Grown, I stood quietly
on an expanse of the Kalahari.
Still. In the redness of sunset,
my breath, the only sound.
A male elephant in musth
drank from a water hole.
He saw his reflection
in the still water between us.
(I saw it too.)
We both stopped
quiet in the glory
of late pink hues.

Living is a balance
of delicate things.

Living an Unsettled Life

*"What brings us to tears,
will also lead us to grace."*

Bob Goff

Flight

To Marilyn, with love.

Sailing above the clouds,
hanging in the sky —
wings across the universe.
Flying free, secure —
it's routine, it seems —

until it isn't,
until the door blows off the plane
from missing screws
and in surprise, tries
to suck the life literally out of us —
or until the plane loses pressure
and oxygen masks drop down
to help us breathe.
Then, it's pretty much every woman
for herself above the clouds.

Life can be like that, and death.

I've lost you to the sky, to the stars.
Your door blew off from Alzheimer's,
the pressure of living with it
sucked life out of you,
took your oxygen,
just as you found the strength
to fly wherever freedom called you.

When the world takes us,
when we are chosen,
we must find new form
so to dance in starlight —
hum and sing to ourselves.
I want to believe
that the universe will know us then,
will be there to affirm our stories,
our prayers for those we've loved on earth —
as we sigh softly, celebrating this life,
and just before our souls
lift us up in peace
and transport us,
through eternity,
to another place and time.

Metamorphosis

diagnosis
I want to feel my life start up again
after my diagnosis, the life-giving
death rays of radiation,
after the stopping of the clock —
that is, cancer.

radiation
cast its shadow on my breast
my lymph nodes, my lung,
missing my heart. Barely.
But it cut deeply into my soul —
silent rays, mutating me.

metamorphosis
all came — cancer came,
fear, the surgeon, radiation came,
and cell death — then,
in new knowing,
life came back, better,
my gratitude — the mutation,
all things asking more of me.

****

To Oncologists
Steven Come, MD & Abram Recht, MD
Stars in my galaxy.

Haiku #3

Parrot plays, sings, rings
his bell, house his, he believes
my soul is his too.

If My Mother

were a book, she'd be a mystery —

pages written by her children —
fill in the blank, connect the dots.
quiet thinker, she was slow to share.

If my mother were a book,
she'd be a mystery —

first chapter, childhood,
descriptive, happy —
later ones, outline only,
no elaboration offered —
marriage, deaths, world war,
marriage again, children,
illness, loss, health, happiness.
The plot kicked her hard at times —
and she'd bury her secrets
deep between the lines.
Her cover did protect her
from life — for life.

From my mother, I learned that —

> * disclosure is an art form — privacy a right.

> * that even if you can't protect your children
>   you can respect and honor them.

* that in living, in sharing,
    everyone needs a place to hide.

*that you can give your children
    the best of yourself —
    values that will serve them.

About questions, feelings —
evasion was usually her go to,
scar tissue her defense.
In time, we'd stop asking
from respect, habit.
She knew shame, sadness, fear —
all barriers to intimacy.
We all have something.
Why the silence?
I never heard her cry.

My mother *was* a mystery —
her story, simple in the telling —
sheltered her complexity.
As mysteries do,
she left us wanting more.

Story complete,
I now study my mother from memory.
I'm getting to know her
through the soft lens of time,
as her reflection melds with my own.

I know her in my touch of things
she left behind,
my feelings sensing hers —
my search, tactile, deliberate,
almost Braille.

From my mother, I learned —

   * that it is the integrity
     of a mother's love
     that is
     the mystery.
     She loves how and as she can.

   She did.

Time is perspective.

Brother

On any given day —
my father did some of the following —

locked our refrigerator,
drank away my mother's wedding rings,
beat whoever was nearest his pain,
made a fearful wife wait by our door —
late nights, to open it for him.
Alcohol. His. Key.
We ran from him, in darkness,
Mother, one child, each hand.

Shock waves, seismic.

My brother told me once —
that I remind him.
Too much. Of his childhood.
That knowing me is painful.
I finally heard him say it.
Can't. Know. You.
                    Can't.

I now understand
his absence from my life.
I get it. Finally.

Self-Preservation.
Comes First.

My reaching
for relationship.
Over.
I feel it.
Closure.

Memory Shackles.

Canyon's Edge

I am standing in strong winds,

       eyes shut tightly
       on the precipice of myself.

It is nearly dark and I cannot breathe —
in or out.

I cannot feel the hemorrhaging of sadness
below the surface of dissociation.

I am waiting for a gust of courage

to carry me

      over the chasm into

          f
          e
          e
          l
          i
          n
          g

Trilogy

Orphan

it was dark under the bed,
but better than being in the world

four years old, alone
seeking safety somewhere.

child of violence
now removed —

from everyone
no one explains

where am I?
I remember, under a bed

in the darkness
innocence not lost

not known.
numb, perhaps for life

forgotten, forgetting —
praying for it, and for sleep

for sleeping very small —
under the bed.

Mother

I am your mother
at four, at seven years,

I held your hand, your brother's,
walking the walk —

up steps to the orphanage door
no words, just feeling —

a final tightening of my hands
over yours

then, "they" took your hands.
I don't know what happened after

(before, when we ran
from your father, I felt alone too)

nine years passed, with visits
then, I married a pedophile —

it let me have you
Him. Too.

Time

adult now, visitor's lounge,
I'm standing in a room, alone
looking out the window, waiting —

when it comes, jolt to the heart
I am four years old again —
feelings, images, deep, known, clear

this room now, was that room then,
years are my markers, decades now
familiar window, repurposed room

bed here then, gone now —
its underbelly and a blanket
were my fortress, home in my darkness

I am the storm, raging
feelings visceral, growing,
but no rain comes, rarely does now

when the world brings you terror —
an unthinkable ungrounding,
and it will —

there is a private space inside,
protected — it is the soul's room,
where each of us will go.

to touch our anguish,
to know it — to stop feeling —
or to let it in,
to accept our mortality

deep pain —
lives unrelenting in this place
It knows no words. Never speaks.

Photo from "the Home,"
Age 8 Years

Centering: Nature's Promise

"No winter lasts forever.
No spring skips its turn."

Hal Borland

Love Song to White Mountain

To Nancy, who gave me Wyoming

Late Summer

Sun setting over White Mountain.
Evening comes to an endless western sky.
Cattle country, and sheep.
I am standing small. Quiet. Alone —
wilderness all around me.
Bitter Creek, Killpecker Creek,
Green River Basin valleys dressed
in ancient shale and sandstone —
in prairie sage. Low grasses.
The earth feels old here and unspoiled.

Evening sky mirrors heaven —
hues of red, orange and pink
embolden shapes above me
as the warm sun of summer
cools. Softens.
I soften with the sky as
azure blues drift from day
into muted darkness.
The sun is setting into me.
Scents are of desert cool, sage,
the delicious perfume of stars

budding silver from ancient spheres
beyond time.

My breath is my rhythm,
as night begins its song.
Songbirds croon evening warnings,
invitations. Their singing
softer in prairie breezes
than in city spaces.
Small animals scatter for shelter,
larger ones will begin the hunt.
Birds here are life's wings.
Mine, as I watch them.

My heart's pulse is solitude.
I am becoming Wyoming.

Early Winter

Once, on this prairie,
I witnessed Basque sheepherders
riding horseback with Great Pyrenees
nudging sheep to graze
their white fur warm and dancing
on skin, icy winds. Nature and herders
are persistent in the cold.

Weather here is a harsh blush
on winter's face,
Herders drive to the rhythm of sheep,
grazing in brisk air. All grace the land
for weeks each year.
Life is prairie, complementing peaks
rising against the sky.

Here, antelope graze green
in the scent of sage.
These Wyoming lands are long known
to generations of herders —
to sons, fathers and grandfather's.
Basque men on horses
are often first to witness early snows —
drifts painted by chilly winds.
Tradition is the language of solitary herders
who know the mountains' secrets.

When night comes to the isolated herders,
it calls the Basque to retreat
to small wooden shelters,
built for hauling by abled horses.
Wooden wheels often navigate miles
of deserted plains, cold winds,
but at night, crackling campfires
warm the herders' bodies, souls.
In the darkness, flames
summon the peace from starry skies.
Under them, herders dream, sheep too,
slumbering in the serenity
of the crisp Wyoming plains.

Basque (Bascos) with Sheep[3]

Midwinter

Overcast. Crisp.
Gusts of chill dance on my cheeks —
life's weathering.
Strands of my hair knot in synchrony
with the earth's whirling air.
I want no hat, needing instead
to be touched by nature's styling.
Wind sculpts everything it touches —
Me too.
But standing coated in winter's air,
my hands seek solace in heavy gloves,
in coat pockets that ease my numbing fingers.
As I wrap my scarf tightly around me,
I widen my stance to remain
standing in place against the gusts.
Beauty is my solitude.
Snow is.
Thoughts are my own.
I am a child of the mountains.
My name is peace.

Early Spring

Snow, high mountains.
God of the north wind,
Boreas, blows his last breath,
covering White Mountain
in one final blanket of snow.

Prairie awakens,
responding in beauty
after winter's desolation.
Lands, seemingly dormant,
are not sleeping,
but are thinking, preparing.

Spring's dance begins,
as the sun remembers,
its fingers touching earth
to thaw the frozen whiteness.
Melting is the snow's crying change.
Tears flow, greeting waiting creeks.
Water dripping, pulsing,
creates nature's rhythm.
Its melody is the happiness
of bird sounds, prairie awakenings.
But in the high country, snow
resists winter's goodbye.
Frozen is its response to change.

In weeks
nests will cradle the eggs
of the season's winged children.
Their parents, hunting,
will bring home
seasonal delicacies.
It is time to exchange
coats for sweaters.
In nature's grace,
spring is returning
to White Mountain.

History of the Basque Sheepherder

To witness the beauty of the Bascos herding sheep, as I have done, brings a gentleness of spirit.

During the 1800's and early 1900's, Basques, or "Bascos," began immigrating from Spain and France, to settle in and around Buffalo, Johnson County, Wyoming. There, they worked the Spanish Ranch and developed a strong reputation for their abilities as sheepherders. As they grew in number, the Basque carved out an economic niche based on their cultural identification. They were known for their skill in herding sheep, several thousands at a time, all on lands in the public domain. In time, this practice of maintaining large herds became controversial among established ranchers and conservationists. Today, some Basque sheepherders still move sheep across the Wyoming plains. Their dogs, Great Pyrenees (or Mastín del Pirineo), move hungry sheep over open spaces.

The "Bascos" were, and are, known for their lifestyle. In years past, Colorado Rocky Ford Enterprise described the Bascos as a people who "naturally take to the life of solitude." For a short time in early spring, the Bascos, on horseback, can be seen herding sheep across the prairies, all weather.

Obituary, Basque Sheepherder[3]

Being in the Delicate

*"There is a period in life when we swallow
knowledge of ourselves and it becomes
either good or sour inside."*

Pearl Bailey

Easter Sunday Massacre

To April

She walked her beagles on the beach
on Cape Cod, was seen playing
with her grandson in the yard.

When later interviewed,
a neighbor said of her —

>*"She kept to herself
>but was nice enough."*

No one suspected it. No one knew —

Until. . .
Easter Sunday
when shots rang out,
across the neighborhood —
when bullets struck their mark —
the bright r—e—d flow of it all
disrupting family dinners.

Until. . .
Gunfire ended Easter egg hunts —
gatherings of laughing children —
in happy innocence, Easter baskets.

(Most did not suspect it.
No one really knew —)

Until. . .
Her photograph appeared
page one, *Boston Globe* —
a battered woman,
in custody and cuffs,
no expression,
eyes blackened and gazing
into the reporter's camera —
her stare rising from a distant place,

And.
Until. . .
beneath the single photo, page one,
the bolded caption read:

> *Physician Kills Husband in Self-Defense.*

Is a picture really worth
a thousand words?
Was her story every really told?

Clarity Is

When whether to leave becomes how to —

when the door swings open and you step boldy through it into the unknown.

That Word

burrowed deep inside me,
sitting like Death. Heavy
on my tongue, my psyche.

Your anger was my silent scream —
as fear of you strangled me.
You were the knee on my throat —
you laughed when I couldn't breathe.

With you, I lived under siege,
knowing your closeted, isolating ways,
paralyzed by your violent obsessions.
I learned silence from you.
W-i-t-h-d-r-a-w-a-l.

Til one day —
in voice and in stance,
it came up strong —
like vomit. Visceral.
That Word. Our Death.

My eyes on yours,
I heard myself say it,
(that word silently rehearsed so often—)

Goodbye.
(Mic drop)

Survivors

those that are,
      choose migration —

moving from violence to wings.

victims, in flight —
      we seek solace, crave peace.

survivors dream to soar —
      never happens when awake.

Closure

To Donna

to end a thing so to go beyond it
with singularity and intent.

to come to terms with loss of relationship
in order to find relationship
on different terms.

to come to oneself through
the mentoring of another who believes
that all lives must find wings.

Scarlet Letter

"Hold thy peace, dear little Pearl —
"We must not always talk in the marketplace
of what happens to us in the forest."

Hester Prynne's mother, *The Scarlet Letter*

Domestic
violence —
a woman scorned
by it — must wear the
mark of one cast aside.
Once she's outed, or outs
herself, she must bear scars,
etched in brain and body, in public,
in herself. Pain, deafening, but silent.

She is a spectacle in red (or any other color),
victim of her life experience, her life choices —
the shame carved deeply into
Her —
by strangers in the marketplace —
sanitized observers, watching from a distance,

who believe Her to be — Unclean.

As Once-Battered Women Do

In court, before the judge
that last day of knowing you,
you glared at me as if to say,

> *"Leave court without protection,*
> *legal or not,*
>
> *"I find you alone, you'll die. Try me."*

I believed you.

Nine months later, living alone,
and having run, in fear,
from court that day —

I look over my shoulder
still waiting to be found —
as once-battered women do.

A-f-t-e-r S-h-o-c-k

Girl friend,
I learned a lot from you.
Loss of your friendship
was a sudden, silent
death of the soul —
at least mine.

Do you remember it —
that night, I said It aloud,
over a martini and dinner?
I was trusting our mood,
our history.

Reciprocity ours —
I had witnessed your successful life,
helped some of it to happen,
knew your unbearable times too.
You'd confided.

I heard you, shared your pain.
You told me how you'd feared new love —
that you were left at the altar,
second wedding, all good.
Strong, aren't we, we said then.

Survivors —
I survived you.

After shock with you, unexpected —
though plenty elsewhere.
But after It, you never called me again,
or returned my calls.

From you, I learned
greater vulnerability,
fear of disclosure
and that trusted friendship —
Sometimes. Isn't. Either. One.

You nurture, invest, give, receive,
but life is fragile.
Loss happens, and change.

Everyone chooses (something).
One leaves.
The other learns.

So. How do I possibly still miss you sometimes?

Inspired by: "All that is dear to me and everyone I love
are of the nature to change. There is no way to escape
being separated from them." — Thich Nhat Hanh[4]

Haiku #4

Hungry feral cats.
Black, furry winter children,
stretching on the porch.

In What Remains

After the fray,
when the violence of a man stops
and the attention of friends
moves on to other things,

a woman spared her life
is left alone
to find herself
in what remains.

In the solitude,
there is a reckoning
with time and place
and a growing of the spirit.

In the subtle quieting of self,
cradled in crisp air,
in autumn light,
hope comes —

slow and new like first snow
on November leaves.
It is the changing of life's seasons
and there is simple joy

in *possibility.*

Waiting for God

When God comes to answer my prayers,

I will ask Her intention in the lessons She has
taught me —

        — about the battering of women

        — about the inequities of poverty,
            homelessness,
            color, culture.

        — even in the mountains.

When God comes down
to answer my prayers,
She will have much to answer for.

****

> *"O-o-h child,*
> *things are gonna get easier*
> *O-o-h child,*
> *things'll get brighter*

some day,
we'll put it together
and we'll get it undone

some day,
when your head is much lighter
some day,
we'll walk in the rays
of a beautiful sun. . .

some day."

The Five Stairsteps
"O-o-h Child"[5]
YouTube.com

To Susanne with Love

To Susanne M.

Only when the sun sits low
in the New England sky
and you brush wind-blown hair
from your Susie eyes,
only when you laugh at our good fortune
(as you often do), do I stop silently
and reflect on the not-so-long-ago.

You take my picture. I take yours.
Sitting on a tall bank of snow,
sunglasses shield us from winter's
late day rays. Friends,
we're sharing memories
on the cameras of our phones.
Lazy Sunday afternoon —

Black Labrador Retriever strolls by unaware —
sand in her toes, sand in ours.
Cool on our faces,
we are happy in snow —
resting ghostlike on the beach.
Blue horizon grows pink and orange.
Sunset nears, evening calm too.

Together, we are sisters
walking in the ocean sand.
We laugh now
as ocean waves lap up
the gleeful sounds we make —
make their own.

But, looking back,
we weren't laughing then —
It is 178 days after
my end to domestic violence —
from the moment you saved me from it.

It is my birthday,

and, miraculously,
we are together
laughing on the beach.

Bird Wings

To Chaco

Living alone again
     and wanting intimacy,
I slip into bed tonight
     to the comfort
of bird's wings
     fluttering gently
as my African Grey
     settles into darkness
on a perch nearby.

Reclamation in Red

To Catherine

Sooner or later, the woman once battered
must move out into life —
a woman of intention

there is a time to step out into Saturday
night — a time to wear the sexy,
flaunt a little cleavage,

a time to remind herself
of how alive she is —
and, though not looking for a man,

that she's still "got *it*."

I wore a cranberry red dress
off the shoulder
right for the dance, for new life.

That night, my conscious act
of reclamation was
my singular entrance
into a black tie affair

at which the right heads turned.

When I Sing

To November

A gentleness of being comes
Saturday morning,
light as sun through my kitchen window,
Grey parrot chatter,
bird toys rattling joyfully
from beak and feathers dancing.

These are the simple sounds of freedom
lyric even in a new home yet unsettled.
Peace lives here, calm
no rage, chaos, or fear of man.

No violence now,
no waiting for anger.
No one lives here to control, to batter.
This is a woman's place,
warm, bathed in morning sun.
I am the only human voice
amid bird wings —
parrot sounds, a joyful noise

Here —
when I am silent, it is by choice
when I *sing*, it is because
I cannot help but sing.

Therapist

settled cross-legged,
comfortable chair —
pen and paper in hand,
you wait patiently near me

for trust
for more disclosure

while, in the shadow
of the Buddha,
I sit quietly near you,
praying for enlightenment.

Dancer

To Barry

You are the dance.
You seem singular among us.

I imagine the whole of you
dancing solo to Tchaikovsky —
moving Brisé, Arabesque
in Sleeping Beauty or Swan Lake —
propelled to adagio, allegro.
Music's crescendo moves you
into Grand je-té or Relevé.

There is no sound, no twirling,
but I imagine you leap,
suspend in air — land quietly
to music I can almost hear.
You are light, body tight, also loose.
You prepare, anticipate,
become art on wings, turning,
with eyes spotting for place.
Delicate shoulders —
arms complement your f-l-o-w.
On stage, black hair up, close —
head your lead, strong, supple neck.
You are toe shoes, satin ribbons —
tightly wrapped on sculpted legs.

Your blistered feet, unseen,
are evidence of will.

Plié, demi-plié, Grand je-té again —
purpose your partner. Perfection too.
Nuance, your dance, is almost play,
mind, body one.
You are goals practiced in measured time.
You are motion on motion.
music's mirror.
Dancer, you are the art we long to know.
To. Be. Body, poetry of swans.
Mind in sync.
Your dance is confidence —
contextual from beginning to end.

Photograph hung over my piano,
I study your image,
moving in my imagination.
You are there — waist down,
black tutu over slender hips.
Frills cover your knees —
moment stopped on point.
In the silence, I can still feel your movement.
The struggle of the dance is familiar.

I also know leaps of faith —
stratospheres of leaping —
ground in shift,
balance a goal.

All dance, in reality, is solo.
Every day is practice.
Even ballerinas fall.

Photo by Barry Currence

Watching the World

"You can observe a lot just by watching."

Yogi Berra

"The Shock of the Old" — Playing Bach and Beethoven's Keyboards[6]

To Joel

The keyboard player
(is) in a state of slight panic

"Why the hell are you doing this?"

Harpsichord, the kind Bach
might have played —
1854 grand pianos housed
at the university's music department,
(and) representing keyboard development
from the seventeenth
to the mid-nineteenth century —
far more temperamental in concert.

(Historic instruments),
they can turn on you,
leave you in the dust.
They can sense your level of stress —
your preoccupation.
They seize up like
some kind of really
mean cat.

As you go up higher —
above middle C,
it gets impossibly bright.
The timbre, curiously unpleasant.
(You) ask yourself —

"Why the hell are you doing this?"

With Beethoven, there's a feeling
of the instrument
starting to buckle under pressure.
Mozart never pushes to that extent.
Beethoven doesn't care —
that's really exciting.

"Music (is) an evolutionary art,
history in motion. . ."

(Blah, Blah)

"Why the hell are you doing this?"

Unrequited Love Defined

The Unrequited.
Live among us, walk among us,
share the subway with us,
and the public parks.
They hang with others who know the lack

of reciprocation or appreciation,
of the loving kind.
Hope comes to the Unrequited in the other's
glance, or stance, or in a chance

meeting where a word or flip of the hair —
is interpreted as something, but is really
something else. When hope does step in
to shake things up, it sets things up —

shuts things down, then sets things up again,
usually to no avail. Love among
the Unrequited is dreamt of, felt,
celebrated, and remembered, but —
is never actually experienced.

The Unrequited know rejection, projection,
dejection, and quiet desperation, until hope
comes again to them, momentarily fulfills,
but then settles, only to tease again.

Haiku #5

Struggling with the world —
"Where have all the flowers gone?"
Violence blossoms.

Peter, Paul & Mary
"Where Have All the Flowers Gone"[7]
YouTube.com

Put Your Lights On

with Jeffrey Woodward

"La ilaha illa Allah" Translation: There is no god but god
Abbreviated lyrics[8] for repetition

"Hey now, all you sinners,
all you lovers. . .
all you killers. . .
all you children. . .
put your lights on,
leave your lights on —
you better leave your lights on
because there's a monster
living under my bed —
whispering in my ear.
There's an angel
with her hand on my head.
She say, I got nothing to fear.
There's a darkness
living deep in my soul.
It's still got a purpose to serve —

so let your light shine
deep into my home.
god, don't let me lose my nerve.

Evening sunlight,
soft pink healing.
Nearby woods settling.
Woodpecker sings his presence —
Reflecting. Him. Us.
Gratitude for being —
Calm. For now. . .

But, dark comes fast.
No light. Hard rain too.
Sometimes, no umbrella.
Turbulence, just is —
In nature, in living on earth.
In being.
Sky is falling. Times are telling.
Turbulence, just is.

George Floyd. Proud Boys.
hate — all crises of the spirit.
Anger Rises up. Palpable.
Un-homed, abandoned. All around.
Everywhere, disconnect the norm.
Therapy to connect, to live.
A I — the question. What is real?
Rhetoric is our song —
but where is Truth?
Where sings calm and caring?
Where do we reflect — live in softness?
Everywhere, disconnect the norm.

All you children,
all you living —
young, parents,
grandparents too —
all genders, ways of loving,
put your lights on.

Monsters roam,
night the cover,
free to claim, to curse.
Night terrors, real,
under the bed. In it.
Who will protect us
from the Wendigo —
from evil?
Monsters roam. Evil does.

Who will lead us through
"the dark night of the soul?"*
We are "lost in oblivion."*
"put your lights on.
put your lights on."*

> "Hey now all you sinners. . .
> All you killers. . .
> All you children. . .
> put your lights on.
> all you children

leave your lights on —

you better leave your lights on
because there's a monster
living under my bed.
whispering in my ear

And there's an angel
with her hand on my head.
She say, I got nothing to fear.

She say, La ilaha illa Allah.
'You shine like stars.

La ilaha illa Allah —
You shine like stars

and we fade away. . .'"

Santana ft. Everlast
"Put Your Lights On"[8]
YouTube.com

Grief Separates[9]

examines, kisses goodbye
a suicided mother —
21st May, my darling —
I thought I was so tough
(but) I'm a timid little soul
myself.

death can cut you off from life —
even when you are still among
the living.
We can never fully say
Goodbye
to those we've loved.
memory can't defend
the dying from death
the(se), the agonies of mind.
and heart.

the children on the harsh winter lawn
are (not playing but) repeating their lament,
suicide (their) burden.
How do we make the best of life and death,
take appropriate measures?

Grief
s-e-p-a-r-a-t-e-s.

Ode to Spirituality

To Sharon

*"Through consciousness, our minds have
the power to change our planet and
ourselves. It is time we heed the wisdom of
the ancient indigenous people and channel
our consciousness and spirit to tend the
garden and not destroy it."*

Bruce Lipton

Indigenous peoples brought us corn,
shared it when we were starving —
first colonies on new lands, not ours.

Spirituality — we claimed it —
said we'd brought it here,
refugees by boat,
stepping onto Plymouth Rock,
then onto lands we christened ours.
For "cause," of course.

Spirituality is not religion,
It is a mindfulness, harmony,
an openness to being.
Acceptance. Receptiveness —
the sharing of the best of us.
for the best of all of us.

Those first days,
spirituality came to us, on foot —
Indigenous people brought us food, seeds,
our hunger fed by their kindness.

Native American Medicine* —
These qualities, *theirs*:

Spirituality is —

"No judgment —
  Light step —
    Peaceful mind —
      Love all creatures —
True tongue —
  Forgiving nature —
    Open heart."

Spirituality came to us,
with the corn, and by example.
And what did we do?

What have we done?

---

*Inspired by: "Native American Medicine — The Eight
Qualities to Develop True Spirituality in Life"

Roulette
with Griot Sabi (Wisdom Amouzou)

"The line, it is drawn.[10]

The curse, it is cast.
The slow one now
will later be fast.
The present now
will later be past
for the times they are a-changin'."

"You'll be drenched to the bone."

Shame leaves a stench,
takes all the prisoners
Didn't learn from it.
Past not past.

It likes the long—term affair,
seeds itself in the womb.
We feed on what mother feeds,
What are you feeding her?

"You'll sink like a stone."

Descend and meet your maker
Present age still willing, able, to induct,
uniform, equip, and slaughter
those whose war it isn't.

All that repression gots to go somewhere,
total eclipse of the heart.
Soul Shock: the inner child
has been waiting —
What are you feeding her?

"For the wheel's still in spin."

She spins as she wills.
The new, the hopeful, and unsuspecting.
No. Won't go.

Only Death calls the numbers.
Some of us been playing roulette too long.
Time to let the dangerous games end.
Operable words,
But with consequences.

"The line, it is drawn.
The curse, it is cast."

Bob Dylan
"The Times They Are a-Changin'"[10]
YouTube.com

Finding Perspective

"Our hearts should do this more."

Hafiz[11]

Touch the Fire

Sometimes, you have to touch the fire,
feel hot flame, know death to embrace life,
nearly drown to learn to swim.
Love can be like that. You touch
the darkness of someone,

then someone else, before
ending that cycle to create a better one.
You burn to find the light, find yourself:
generate oxygen, light your own flame.
You learn healthy is a choice —

to give from your best self, not your needy one.
Sometimes, you have to touch
the fire, feel hot flame, know the burn.
Fear can be like that —
It convinces you that you are alone —

you stumble, choose history over possibility.
Fear finds you in your dreams,
shakes you, wakes you.
You want more and better,
but more of what —
of what's expected?

You want change,
but change can be a fear monger.

Fear of it, relieved,
is the Phoenix rising from the ashes.
Sometimes, you have to touch the fire —

to feel something, sometimes anything —
to learn why, become whole,
find legs, wings, walk or fly.
Living is like that. You carry your baggage
through the flames —

looking for someone to leave it with.
Gets heavy. You can leave it,
but not with anyone else. They have their own.
You have to feel the burn, the fear, sadness,
before joy comes.

Fire chars,
     shapes,
          purifies,
               hurts —

makes way for
new growth.

The forest knows this,
and the heart.

*"And life flows on within you
and without you."*

George Harrison[12]

The Beatles
"Within You Without You"[12]
YouTube.com

Endnotes

1   Rainer Maria Rilke, "Go to the limits of your longing," in *Rilke's book of hours: Love poems to God*, trans. Anita Barrows and Joanna Macy (Riverhead Books, 2005), 119.

2   Frederick Buechner, "Grace," in *Wishful Thinking: a theological ABC* (Harper & Row, 1973)

3   Photos courtesy of Dr. Jim Connors, "Basque Sheepherders in the American West," in *The Friday Footnote*, October 22, 2021

4   Thich Nhat Hanh, *The Heart of the Buddha's Teaching* (Harmony Books, 2015), 124.

5   Stan Vincent, "O-o-h Child," on *Stairsteps*, Five Stairsteps (Buddah, 1970). #402 on *Rolling Stone* magazine's 500 Greatest Songs of All Time.

6   Erasure Poem. Original text: Alex Ross, "The Shock of the Old," in *The New Yorker*, November 21, 2022, 70-71.

7   Pete Seeger and Joe Hickerson, "Where Have All the Flowers Gone?" on *Peter, Paul and Mary*, Peter, Paul and Mary (Warner Bros. 1962). Song chosen as one of the "Top 20 Political Songs" by *New Statesman*, 2010

8   Erik Shrody, "Put Your Lights On," on *Supernatural*, Carlos Santana with Everlast (Arista, 1999)

9   Erasure Poem. Original text: Hilton Als, "The Gentleman," in *The New Yorker*, June 6, 2022, 57-62.

10 Bob Dylan, "The Times They Are a-Changin'," on *The Times They Are a-Changin'*, Bob Dylan (Columbia, 1965)

11 Hafiz, "Our Hearts Should Do This More," *The Gift: Poems by Hafiz*, trans. Daniel Ladinsky. (Penguin Compass, 1999), 91.

12 George Harrison, "Within You Without You," on *Sgt. Pepper's Lonely Hearts Club Band*, The Beatles (EMI, 1967)

Acknowledgements

Gratitude to —

The Community Literature Initiative (CLI) in Los Angeles, California, Hiram Sims and staff. Thanks to the Poetry Publishing Program for guidance in the initial manuscript completion, especially Laura Joy Clarke, Kayla Toris, and Kimberly James.

Production Editor Emily Anne Evans, whose skill set enhanced this publication in many visible and thoughtful ways. Your work integrity is of the highest level.

Poet/Teachers Marissa Forbes, Andrés Sánchez and Rolanda Simmons for your expertise and creativity, and for teaching by example.

The Colorado-Wyoming and National Chapters of the Community Literature Initiative for enhancing my experience with poetry and for bringing me to a wonderful community of poets.

Wisdom Amouzou, Griot Sabi, talented creative, poet and visual artist, who co-wrote the poem, "Roulette," shared in this collection.

Exceptional poets Ahja Fox, María Toloché (Zelina Gaytan), Jessica Gnoza, Allison Jasinski, Robbie Robinson, Cecily Stone, and Marie Timbreza for your creativity, talent, and inspiration.

Ronald Reed Sill. I appreciate your generosity in allowing me the use of your artwork for the front cover.

Most importantly, Jeffrey Woodward for who you are, and for our work together. Thank you for your poem, "And She Planted Her Poetry Everywhere," which begins this collection, and for our collaboration on the poem, "Put Your Lights On."

About the Author

Peg Codding (Ph.D) is a Board-Certified Music Therapist (MT-BC) who uses music, movement, and research in academic and clinical settings. She has been creating poetry for years and further developed her writing through her affiliation with the Community Literature Initiative based in Los Angeles. She has also taught Floology, original poetry combined with live musical improvisation, among musicians. Peg is a certified storyteller, working with the expressive telling of stories to young children in Colorado Public Schools (spellbinders.org).

Peg's first collection of poetry is entitled *Balance of Delicate Things*. Her poetry was also published in the anthology *Welcoming the Muse: Meta and Other Forms* (Twenty Bellows, 2024). A Colorado native, Peg returned to the mountains after years of living in flat lands across the country. The mountains have always been at the center of her soul. They now surround her.